Dr. Sandy Burket
life of an Overcom.... ....
personally learned how to move from victim to overcomer and have joy. Her character and anointing of
joy do not waver with the challenges she experienced
in the past and the present. She has a revelation, from
God, that kingdom joy is to be the backbone of one's
life. Joy is not an emotion of happiness but a knowing
that God already has a plan on how to walk in a life
of joy even though the heart is full of pain.

Her life mission is to be used by God to bring
healing to the brokenhearted, to equip the saints, and
to help them fulfill their destinies. She believes that
a healed past becomes a testimony that launches one
into their life purpose. Sandy relies on the Holy Spirit
for revelations that direct individuals to know how
to activate God's truth. Biblical truth moves individuals from being a victim to being an overcomer full
of laughter and hope. Through life experiences and
spiritual wisdom, she has taught thousands of individuals in the states and internationally that victory
from painful events is obtainable.

It is a blessing to have Dr. Sandy ordained in the
Christian International Network. Early on in our
relationship, I recognized even though she is short,
she is a stick of dynamite in a darkened world.

God bless you Dr. Sandy for sharing your years of
extensive research, over 40 years of writing, teaching,
and training that have made you the effective minister
of human transformation that you are today. May
thousands of Saints and Ministers of Jesus Christ

receive transformation through the truths in this book so that they can fulfill God's highest calling for mankind. Being conformed to the character, image, and ministry of God's Son Jesus Christ is God's highest calling in all Saints and Christian Ministers. Romans 8:29, 2 Corinthians 3:18

—Bishop Bill Hamon
Bishop, Christian International Apostolic-Global Network and Author of *The Eternal Church, Prophets & Personal Prophecy,* and other books

Dr. Sandy Burkett is a gifted communicator of a life message that sets persons free to live life as the Creator intended. Her insights, into human behavior, are imparted with wisdom and compassion. Oliver Wendell Holmes, Sr. said, "Many people die with their music still in them." Dr. Burkett's mission is to assure each of us there is a fruitful pursuit of "unending joy" for the overcomer who "sings" their song.

—Bishop Joseph L. Garlington, Sr.
Presiding Bishop of Reconciliation Ministries International and President of Bishop Joseph Garlington Ministries

We have known Dr. Sandy Burkett for 28 years. First we served her as interpreters, later we hosted her at numerous conferences and events in Ukraine. Each time she writes or teaches we always find it relevant, profound, applicable. We consider it a blessing to know her and be able to draw from the well of practical wisdom she is so willing to share.

—Maksym and Yuliya Bilousov
Pastors of Dnipro Christian Church

The Lie Your Life Is Based On dives deep into understanding why we choose to live the way we do following trauma and difficult experiences in life. Dr. Sandy Burkett is an overcomer, and she invites us to learn how to walk in healing, through our battles, with Christ at the center. This book examines the life of an overcomer as the Scripture teaches, and how to recognize the pitfalls of believing lies from our past experiences. It's a must-read as we learn to walk in wholeness.

—Apostle Bill Themelaras
Senior Leader of Oasis City Church and
Covenant Church of Pittsburgh and Author of
*Voice-Activated: How to Discover Your Identity,
Define Your Life, and Declare Your Future*

In *The Lie Your Life Is Built On*, Sandy Burkett does an incredible job providing a blueprint for freedom and transformation. Her experience from decades as a counselor and minister of the gospel combine to provide both practical wisdom and proven techniques which will produce the testimonies of individuals who have triumphed over trauma and tragedy and now live as Overcomers. As you read, you will be changed!

—Jane Hamon

Proverbs speaks about the building process. It requires wisdom, knowledge, understanding and discernment. Too often we're clueless about these building blocks, finding the first available "fix" to solve personal issues and heal our emotional pain. Often we believe it's just the devil. Sandy Burkett has so clearly, eloquently, and understandably addressed the challenge of moving from an identity as victim to survivor and ultimately overcomer using the building blocks the book of Proverbs outlines. I found her explanations and style refreshing and eye opening. I'm looking forward to getting my personal copy of this book. I highly recommend this book.

—Barbara J. Yoder

THE LIE YOUR LIFE IS BUILT ON

EXPERIENCE UNENDING JOY

SANDY BURKETT, PHD.

ethos
collective

Printed in the United States of America.

Published by Ethos Collective™
PO Box 43, Powell, OH 43065

EthosCollective.vip

Library of Congress Cataloging: 20229244040
Softcover: ISBN: 978-1-63680-113-1
Hardcover: ISBN: 978-1-63680-114-8
Ebook: ISBN:978-1-63680-115-5

Available in hardcover, softcover, ebook, and audiobook.

To protect the privacy of those who have shared their stories with the author, some details and names have been changed. Any Internet addresses (websites, blogs, etc.) and telephone numbers printed in this book are offered as a resource. They are not intended in any way to be or imply an endorsement by Ethos Collective, nor does Ethos Collective vouch for the content of these sites and numbers for the life of this book.

Unless otherwise noted, all Scripture quotations are taken from the HOLY BIBLE, NEW INTERNATIONAL VERSION®. NIV®. Copyright ©1973, 1978, 1984 by International Bible Society. Used by permission of Zondervan. All rights reserved.

Scripture quotations marked NASB are taken from the New American Standard Bible®, Copyright © 1960, 1962, 1963, 1968, 1971, 1972, 1973,1975, 1977, 1995 by The Lockman Foundation. Used by permission." (www.Lockman.org)

Scripture quotations noted KJV are from The Holy Bible, KING JAMES VERSION.

The Holy Bible English Standard Version, ESV Text edition 2016 Crossway Bible a publishing company ministry of Good News Publisher.

DEDICATION

This book is dedicated to my husband Greg,
who is an example of one who has moved
from victim to overcomer.

CONTENTS

FOREWORD

When you meet someone new you don't know what to expect. Such was the case on that August afternoon. Our mutual friend Rob Kopp told me I should connect with Dr. Sandy Burkett. I'm so glad I did. Immediately, I noticed her fire. As the CEO of a company called Igniting Souls, I tend to spot passion, commitment, and resolve in others rather quickly.

The rest of our time together that day, I happily sat in the role of learner. Despite having several advanced theological decrees, I was sincerely impressed with her ability to break down deep spiritual topics into simple and practical applications.

Dr. Sandy has a gift. In this book you'll see that gift. Through her discovery, The Journey to Unending Joy™, she leads us from Victim and Survivor to Overcomer. It's one of the best explanations of the human struggle we all know too well.

Within her book you'll see yourself. But even more importantly, you'll see who God created you to be. In that picture you'll confront a choice. You can ignore the truth or you can let the truth set you free.

I choose freedom. Thank you Dr. Sandy for letting God use you to show us the way.

—Dr. Kary Oberbrunner, *Wall Street Journal* and *USA Today* bestselling author

I'M A SURVIVOR

What I feared has come upon me; what I dreaded has happened to me. I have no peace, no quietness. I have no rest, but only turmoil.

—Job 3:25-26 (New International Version)

Victim. Survivor. Overcomer.

Three words we often use to describe ourselves after we've experienced an event of some difficulty or a traumatic experience of some kind. Society will tell us these three words are synonymous, but they are not. While we often use them interchangeably, there are important distinctions to make and explore.

- A *victim* is described as "a person harmed or injured as a result of a crime, accident, or another event."
- A *survivor* is defined simply as "a person who survives."
- An *overcomer* is known as "one who succeeds in dealing with or gaining control over a problem or difficulty."

While the differences in these definitions are slight, how we choose to define ourselves matters. Review the Journey to Unending Joy™ chart. Compare and contrast each category. For the rest of this book we'll unpack what this means and the freedom that's available to every child of God.

Victim	Survivor	Overcomer
"I won't grow up"	"I'm a survivor"	"I shall overcome"
Drowning in Water	Treading in Water	Walking on Water
Living Dead	Life	Abundant Life
Unprotected	Self-Protected	Protected
Orphan	Step Child	Adopted Son or Daughter
Ghetto	Suburbs	Palace
Past	Future	Present
Child	Teenager	Adult
Not able to love	Too busy to love	Able to love unconditionally
Unforgiveness	Acceptance	Forgiveness
Generational Curses	Personal Achievements	Spiritual Inheritance
Never Dreams	Sometimes Dreams	Always Dreams
Poor	Middle Class	Royalty
Loner	Lonely	Never Alone
Lie	Half Truth	Truth
Situational Joy	Happiness	Unending Joy

HOW IT ALL BEGINS

After we experience something traumatic, part of our identity becomes *victims.* Something has happened to us or has been done to us that permanently alters the way we see the world and the ways in which we react to it. Acknowledging this victimization is the first step in healing and moving toward becoming an overcomer.

A survivor's identity is a step further than a victim's. Survivors have taken action to acknowledge the trauma and work to heal—developing their own coping skills. Most people will stop here at a survivor identity, and say "that's enough for me, I've survived the event and moved forward." Yet some of those coping methods block survivors from becoming overcomers. As this book will display, accepting a survivor's identity will always be second best to graduating to an overcomer.

What does it mean to be an overcomer? We hear the terms *victim* and *survivor* often enough in day-to-day life, so they feel familiar and identifiable to us. *Overcomer* is a much lesser known term, yet it is the most important identity we should seek after a trial in our lives. Overcomer is synonymous with being victorious, prevailing, and conquering—much more than merely surviving. The Bible tells us, "I am convinced that any suffering we endure is less than nothing compared to the magnitude of glory that is about to be unveiled within us." (Romans 8:37, The Passion Translation).

Sounds pretty sweet, right?

Yet unlike being a victim or a survivor, to become an overcomer we need help. The only way to truly overcome is to invite the Holy Spirit into our hearts and allow God to guide us into overcoming our battles. It is only through trust and faith that we can learn to truly overcome what has continually haunted us. His light enables us to escape the darkness.

Before we reach overcomer status, though, we all have to return to the beginning and understand what it means to be a victim. The key aspect of a victim's identity is understanding that the past unhealed wounds will be transferred onto the present relationships in one's life. Transference explains why someone is in a state of victimhood, but it also provides clarity on the actions that follow traumas. It is important to learn about transference so we can recognize it in our friends, families, and peers and help them to see it as well.

WHY WE STAY STUCK

Have you ever wondered why individuals enter into cycles of the same types of painful events? Why do people leave a dysfunctional relationship simply to enter into a new, equally dysfunctional one? Why do some people bounce from one job or one church to another? All of us know friends, family, coworkers, and neighbors who fit into these descriptions. Perhaps we've noticed they are restless, or anxious. Or perhaps instead of being anxious, we've noticed they are incredibly eager to step into various roles to please the new people they've met. There are a plethora of reasons why the people we love behave this way, but in order to understand them, we first need to ask some questions. These questions are worth asking, and the answers can be found in recognizing cycles of transference.

Transference is a phenomenon denoted by the unconscious redirection of feelings from one person or place to another. Transference is one of the most common experiences, yet it is also one of the most overlooked mechanisms of dysfunctional behavior. In our examples above, we see the cyclical nature of transference in the painful circles people run in, and often, they have no understanding that they are running in circles at all.

Transference is created from repressed thoughts, sensations, memories, or perception of reality. Repression is a coping mechanism that is learned as a child. The capacity of the child to repress emotions and memories is used as a coping tool for survival. Therefore a pattern is developed where the adult cannot separate what is healthy from what is unhealthy; what is childhood truth or false perception. When these areas are repressed, the plumb line of "what is healthy" becomes distorted. The ability to "feel appropriately" also becomes distorted when we walk in excessive repression. Individuals who walk in the pattern of repression are more likely to transfer their issues onto others than those who face and deal with life's unpleasant events

Take, for example, your sister Sarah, who seems unable to find a significant other who is consistently kind to her. Each new person she meets, she genuinely believes will be the last one, yet when the relationship fails, she finds another that fulfills her beliefs and continues to a cycle of dysfunction. Your sister isn't even aware she is stuck in this cycle. Rather, she's only aware that, each time she finds a new significant other, she is trying to make that person love her.

Transference is a desperate attempt by one's subconscious to bring temporary relief from the pain or anxiety of unsatisfied needs, unhealed conflict, or emotional trauma. This desire for relief subconsciously produces a cycle of victimization in which the victim blames, manipulates, and makes unreasonable demands of others. They project the emotions and beliefs from their past to the present situation.

Consider Sarah again. This time, the man she is dating has unresolved trauma in the area of abandonment—perhaps his mother left when he was a child. The man, we'll call him Jake, grew up with a constant fear of being left and was raised by a father who wasn't emotionally available as someone to comfort, encourage, or allow his son to experience the father's love. Thus, Jake learned to handle his fear of abandonment by making sure he never allowed anyone to become close to him emotionally. In order to avoid abandonment, he would leave a relationship whenever he began to feel that emotional connection.

Now, let's say Jake is dating your sister, who he genuinely likes and feels a strong connection with. Jake and your sister are both caught in cycles of transference. They are drawn to each other because victims marry victims. Jake will leave your sister so she never has the opportunity to leave him, and your sister will start her cycle all over again with a new significant other.

Jake left to momentarily alleviate the fear of the trauma he never truly faced, but he never handled the trauma itself. When one is in the midst of transferring the past onto the present they become like the "sow that is washed [going] back to wallowing in the mud" (2 Peter 2:22). Thus, they recreate their trauma experience, as Jake does when he leaves a healthy relationship for seemingly no reason at all.

TRANSFERENCE LOVES TRIGGERS

If transference is so common but also so unheard of, how do we recognize it? We can spot transference by looking for a *trigger*: an event or occurrence that sets off a negative emotional response concerning a present event that bears similarities to a previous event. Generally, the most painful triggers are seen in relation to negative events that occurred in childhood—for example, Jake, who experienced childhood abandonment at a young age. In early childhood events, the emotional response tends to become foundational, consciously or unconsciously, to who that person becomes as an adult. His beliefs create negative emotional responses.

We can think of these trigger moments as sunburns. The original burn is painful, but if you put that burn back into the sun, the pain is suddenly amplified. Trigger events work the same way. For Jake, dating your sister is likely a trigger event, a recurrence that activates the subconscious and conscious beliefs and emotions of past trauma. In both events, Jake is faced with a situation that initially feels safe, comforting, and beneficial to his well-being. Both instances also involve women he looks up to and respects. His mother's leaving has been ingrained deeply in his subconscious, and he now believes that Sarah will leave him in the same way. His relationship with Sarah is like an emotional yo-yo. He is either hot or cold. Any future positive and stable relationship with a woman will likely be a trigger event for Jake until he addresses the core of the problem.

These unconscious feelings take root in the subconscious and can negatively influence our judgments, inner vows, and personal goals that take away from our ability to be an overcomer. It's important to note that triggers are not demonic in nature, but rather stem from unhealed childhood traumas. Jake isn't an awful person because he has trauma he needs to face. He simply needs someone to help him to recognize his transference, and that someone is God. Many times God uses others to reveal truth in one's life. He's an awesome, loving God who allows us to experience these triggers and uses them to bring us out of these repetitive cycles.

Transference always takes place when there is a combination of mutual trust and authority. Jake and your sister Sarah have established a sense of mutual trust with one another and feel as though they have a good amount of authority or at least input in the decisions that the other makes. However, any relationship that resembles a parent/child or leader/follower relationship is vulnerable due to an inherent imbalance of power. An imbalance of power may be occurring between your sister and Jake. Jake is constantly, whether consciously or unconsciously not, trying to keep an upper hand in the relationship to protect himself emotionally. This, too, is a kind of transference as well, that whoever has more power in a relationship has full authority rather than balanced authority.

When there is a healthy power dynamic, individuals in the parent or leader role can often walk beside those who are brokenhearted. When authority is used properly, phenomenal mentor relationships can be created and healthy relationships can be fostered. A wonderful example of this is God's relationship with us—there is a distinct imbalance of power, but it is used only for our good. Unlike us, God has only the kindest intentions at heart and longs to mentor us to be more like him.

TRANSFERENCE IS AS OLD AND TIME

Transference isn't a new idea. There are many instances of it in the Biblical stories we know well. We see it as early as Eden with Adam and Eve blame shifting when God asks about their sin.

Centuries later, in 1 Samuel 30:1-31 NIV, we find a striking example of transference. In these passages,

King David and his men suffered a terrible shock. While they were fighting a battle, the Amalekites destroyed their homes and took captive their wives and children. They probably expected a warm welcome upon their arrival, but instead found everything close to them had been seized or demolished.

David and his army were overcome with grief and anger, for the scripture says they "wept until they had no strength left to weep" (1 Samuel 30:4 NIV). Rather than confronting the issue at hand, the soldiers turned David into their emotional scapegoat. These men transferred their beliefs, judgments, and emotional pain onto David when they experienced the loss of family and possessions. David's army consisted of men who never took the time to be healed of their past, thus the past accompanied them into battle. David was surrounded by wounded people. 1 Samuel 22:2 NIV states, "All those who were in distress or depressed or discontented gathered around him, and he became their leader." God fostered a healthy relationship with David that positioned him as a leader.

PAIN MANAGEMENT THROUGH PROJECTION

In the same way, men and women today try to manage their pain in unhealthy ways by pushing their feelings onto others. Projection is transferring what you feel onto another person to avoid pain and validate your emotions. When a person projects what they believe or feel about themselves onto someone else, they will, consciously or unconsciously, expect a response that affirms that belief or feeling.

For example, imagine a person tells you that they know you are angry with them. They are actually telling you they are angry with themselves. Their projection often initiates a response of justification or explaining oneself from you. The hope is that your response will be one of reassurance, comfort, or instruction.

If resentment has taken root in the person, they wait for a negative response. This negative response will serve to confirm and validate their own reasons for rejecting their parents. The problem is that those who project the issues of their soul onto others will most likely misread the responses of others. An example of this would be the conclusion that "you must hate me." The reality may be that the person actually hates themselves and projects this feeling

Consider your sister. She is stuck in a cycle searching for validation, repeatedly projecting how she feels about herself (insecure, unlovable) onto the man she is dating, and thus, waiting for him to validate how she feels. Projection is a continual circle of victimization, nearly impossible to stop until it is pointed out.

RESISTANCE IS FUTILE AND HARMFUL

When you confront a person with transference or projection issues, you will likely encounter resistance. Resistance comes when a person does not want to face the reality of deprivations, painful memories, or overwhelming emotions. Their impulse is to avoid pain by preserving a measure of "unreality" in their soul. The fantasy that was created (and probably lived with for many years) are expressed in the form of resistance. It is a cognitive defense against dealing with memories and emotions which spans from both unconscious and conscious realms of the soul.

Pride enables those with transference issues to resist taking responsibility for sinful responses to past events instead of dealing with how the event has affected them. When pride is in the heart, we cannot accept instruction from someone else about what is true. Pride blocks our capacity to receive insight from God concerning the matters of our own heart. Pride not only fights against the truth of the past, but it also holds back the grace God longs to extend (see Psalms 81: 10-16 NASB).

TRANSFERENCE OFTEN SHOWS UP AT CHURCH

Transference of unhealed events are seen in every relationship in life. This creates a cycle of continual victimization. Transference is commonly found in church settings because of the relationships built in that community. Trust is established between leaders of the church and church attendees—the spiritual leaders in the church take on a parental role for the people who attend and use that role to help mentor those who are hurting. At the beginning of these relationships, a balance exists between the two as the leader mentors the church-goer in a parental fashion. Yet over time, the church-goer begins to transfer their emotions and expectations onto the church leader.

The attendee begins to carry an expectation that the leader will treat them the same way that their parents treated them. Regardless of whether the attendee experienced a healthy or unhealthy parental situation, it is not healthy for the person seeking help to project their expectations onto the leader instead of allowing the leader to help.

Let's say that Jake is attending church again, hoping to find a spiritual leader to guide him. He is referred to Anne, a counselor in the church, and they begin working through some of his issues. At first, Jake feels his connection with God is growing stronger and it's better than it was before. He's finally getting to the root of the problems he's been grappling with. Over time, though, Jake begins to pull away without knowing why. The reason for this, of course, is that Jake has started to transfer his experience with his mother onto Anne, the new parental figure in his life. Anne has done nothing to indicate she is going to abandon Jake, but because the trigger issue has not been addressed, Jake has succumbed to his fears and used his defense tactics to push away the help she has offered.

In churches, we see these mentor/mentee roles, and with them often comes transference. Learning to recognize transference can help restore solid, faith-based relationships between church leadership and those seeking solace in the church.

TRANSFERENCE WITHIN MARRIAGE

When two believers in Christ come for marriage counseling, we frequently see issues of transference in their union. An individual may marry a person whose characteristics mirror those of a parent. Sarah, for example, has a demanding mother whom she is always seeking validation from. This experience transfers over into the relationships that she seeks with potential husbands. These men are often like her mother (difficult to please, demanding, and so on). Many times, the person will choose a marital partner who shares characteristics to the parent with whom they had the most difficult relationship. They may not have recognized these similarities during their time of dating, but after a period of time in marriage their "old tapes begin to play." These old tapes are the bitter, rooted judgments and inner vows made during painful childhood events which trigger the repetitive cycle.

For Sarah, marriage would initially be considered a victory—she will have exited the cycle of jumping from relationship to relationship due to her past traumas. Perhaps her husband will not be like Jake, meaning he is willing to stick around and work to make the relationship successful. What Sarah does not see, however, is that her husband is cultivating a relationship similar to that which she shares with her father. She has not yet addressed her insecurity in any meaningful way. And so, she continues to project and transfer in her new marriage. When transference is part of marriage conflict, one party often believes they are in a no-win situation, and the reality is that they are. The conflict is not caused by present-day events, rather the unhealed wounds brought into the conflict by the offending partner. Subconsciously, the person is trying to rectify their childhood experience, but instead produces self-inflicted pain and wounds the spouse.

Sarah and Jake both have deeply rooted, traumatic experiences that they went through in their childhood. For Jake, it is the fear of abandonment. For Sarah, it is the need for approval. As adults, each is seeking something from other individuals rather than help from God to heal themselves. These are just two examples of transference, with Jake and Sarah representing what many go through on a daily basis.

Jake and Sarah are both in victim identities at this point in their life. Their cycles of transference, projection, and rejection have not yet been pointed out to them. They long to move from victim to survivor but haven't yet understood how they are stuck in the victim stage. Jake and Sarah must recognize their defensive instincts and consciously push against them to move to the next stage.

With the help of others, moving from victim to survivor is a manageable step. Once taken, we can begin to consider why we accept victim and survivor titles instead of the best option: being an overcomer.

1

TOO EASILY PLEASED

It would seem that Our Lord finds our desires not too strong, but too weak. We are half-hearted creatures, fooling about with drink and sex and ambition when infinite joy is offered us, like an ignorant child who wants to go on making mud pies in a slum because he cannot imagine what is meant by the offer of a holiday at the sea. We are far too easily pleased.

—C. S. Lewis

Let's take a deeper dive into victims and survivors. Frankly, we live in a survivor culture, one that glorifies the suffering we have experienced. Society invites us to conquer our pain alone in the most efficient way possible. Trauma is often embedded deeply into our identity and worn as a badge of honor, to be carried around proudly, just beneath the surface. We can puff out our chests and brag about the pain we overcame. Being a survivor is trendy, something we applaud and aspire to become.

We celebrate people who identify as victims and survivors. We romanticize the idea of climbing out of difficult circumstances. The journey from victim to survivor is arduous, and thus, when victims reach the finish line of this transition, they tend to want to stop. In their minds, they have fought an heroic battle and now they've completed their healing journey. Society often views survivors in a positive light. They are encouraged and validated. Being a victim isn't a bad thing, nor is being a survivor. These identities are fluid states. We might be a victim in one area and a survivor in another. For example, when you go home during a holiday do you respond to the family as a victim? Yet in other relationships you respond as an overcomer. During conflicts when you respond as a victim you are demonstrating childishness. When a survivor is trying to resolve conflict, that demonstrates double-mindedness. They change the rules, and thus, conflict is not resolved. When you respond as an overcomer, you demonstrate being an adult. When there is ongoing conflict in a relationship it is because both individuals move back and forth as a victim or survivor. Perhaps you are a victim in your relationship with your sister, an overcomer in your struggles with addiction, and a survivor of an accident causing PTSD. All three areas require different journeys from one state to another, and being in any one of them is fine as long as we work toward being overcomers.

SONGS OF SURVIVORS

Survivors have an interesting and positive connotation in contemporary society.

Each generation looks at surviving a little differently. We can see this in mainstream music, from pop to country to rap. Take Destiny's Child, for example. Their song, "I'm a Survivor," talks about pushing through trauma and moving forward on your own by working harder and hustling.

This idea is pervasive—that we are entirely responsible for our own healing and success and it is a badge of honor to overcome difficulties. We see this common thread in younger generations, largely due to an individualistic culture that society has popularized. The younger generation feels the need to conquer their trauma alone, which results in transference. Jake and Sarah would fall in this category—they both are struggling with their pasts and are failing to find that imaginary badge of honor received once overcoming trauma.

But baby boomers don't get a pass. They share a similar idea, evidenced in songs from their day, including "I Will Survive" by Gloria Gayner. Every generation focuses on what they have done rather than what has been done for them. This is an example of how unhealed wounds cause us to live in our own world order.

The lie is that you're a survivor, and that's all you'll ever be. Songs have been sung about this from generation to generation, from Gloria to Beyoncé.

As we try to move from identity to identity, we find ourselves becoming absorbed in what *we* are able to accomplish, how much *we* are able to find healing and fulfillment. While it is true that no matter what space of our spiritual journey we find ourselves in is wrong, we need to look outward to God to move forward into becoming an overcomer.

MORE IN STORE

C. S. Lewis exhorts us to reject the title of a survivor as the representative end of our spiritual journey in healing. We have a more powerful calling. Popular culture pushes the idea of survivor, to have experienced trauma and to have conquered it. But conquering past traumas and fully healing from them are two very different issues. Society tells us that pushing forward and moving on is the way to go, and that doing everything the best way you know how is admirable and should be celebrated. C. S. Lewis tells us that by remaining in those moments, we are too easily pleased.

What does Lewis's quote mean in terms of our present survivor culture? Simply put, we are content with the label of survivor and nothing else. We are satisfied putting our identity into what we have survived and nothing more. C. S. Lewis compared this thinking to being content making mud pies in the slum when there is an entire ocean available for our taking. The ocean is metaphorical for what God has to offer us when we put our identity into him rather than into ourselves. God removes the label of "survivor" so we stop focusing on what we have accomplished and see what he has done for us. Modern survivor culture clashes with God's desire for us to lean into him. By accepting how God sees us, we can choose loftier goals than merely surviving.

The first step to moving from a survivor mindset to an overcomer mindset is to recognize that we are not asking for enough. Our loving God offers abundant life, more than we could ever imagine. The key is that we must ask for it.

2

THE BARN IS BURNING

I will be Father to you, and you will be my sons and daughters, says the Lord Almighty.

—2 Corinthians 6:18 ESV

We are too easily pleased, sculpting our survivor identity to be our entire story, but at the same time, we focus on things that ultimately do not help us understand and grow from our trauma. We turn to comforting habits, such as meditation and memorizing scripture, but nothing changes. We put ourselves in a barn, feeling safe within four walls. Our identity slowly becomes all about the works that we are doing, not what has already been done for us. This is where one puts their nose to their navel and walks in introspection instead of submitting to the Holy Spirit. When one allows the Holy Spirit to reveal the problem, one changes on the inside.

We focus on what we can do. This is a survivor mentality and it forces our hearts to fall into the wrong places. When we accept the adoption God offers, we can leave our barns and enter the alternative: the Kingdom of God. Before this takes place let's reexamine where we are before we accept our adoption.

Let's consider Sarah again. Perhaps someone points out to her that she's trapped in a cycle of transference, and she decides she is too easily pleased living life as a survivor. Now that Sarah recognizes this cycle, she may begin to build walls around herself with things that bring her comfort and security. Let's say she puts up one wall for exercise and another for self-help books. Two more walls go up for picking a church and getting involved in the worship team. Continuing the metaphor, maybe Sarah fills her "barn" with "hay and animals" like journaling and sewing. All of these items bring great comfort to Sarah and make her feel as though she is achieving and making positive, progressive changes in her life that will lead her ultimately to healing.

The issue, of course, is that Sarah is still outwardly focused rather than internally focused. Sarah is resisting the option of adoption. She is building a barn around herself that provides physical stability in life, but doesn't help her heal from the hurt she has experienced in the past. To figure out how to work toward that healing, Sarah needs to ask the Holy Spirit to reveal past memories that established the cycles of her life. The first step is to trust and accept the Holy Spirit. (For information on how to trust and accept the Holy Spirit, see Appendix.)

A survivor has one of four types of hearts. Each heart is indicative of a different struggle in the path from survivor to overcomer.

THE ORPHAN HEART

Orphan hearts are characterized by harboring a deep bitterness, projecting their wounds onto others, and using poor coping mechanisms to attempt to feel better. Orphan-hearted people are victims who still fear their trauma. Webster's dictionary defines an orphan as one that both parents died or the absence of one parent. Children who have a relationship with only one parent may be considered an orphan, much as we have seen happen in Jake's childhood.

Leif Hetland in his book, *Healing the Orphan Spirit*, has a great description of an orphan's heart. "It is a place of the soul hidden away, held back and not yielded to the Lordship of Jesus Christ. It is a secret place of the soul with the door closed and you are the only one with a key." The black hole is filled with despair, hopelessness, and helplessness. Orphans live as victims believing God has abandoned them and He is the creator of their pain.

Jake has an orphan heart. He projects his wounds onto Sarah when he assumes that she is going to abandon him without giving her an opportunity to prove otherwise. Instead of facing his deeply rooted trust issues, he abuses his power by dating women only to leave them with the excuse that he is protecting himself. In reality, he is making excuses to hurt others in the same way he was hurt. All of this, of course, is because Jake still fears his trauma of being abandoned, and he has not allowed the adoption of the Holy Spirit.

THE STEPCHILD HEART

People with stepchild hearts always feel that they don't truly fit in. A stepchild's heart may be the result of a relationship with only one parent or living in a family where siblings are favored. As a result, they're constantly moving from one group to another in search of validation. Survivors with these hearts are looking for a sense of belonging. Sarah has a stepchild's heart. She continually looks to the person she is dating for validation and a sense of belonging. Sarah feels that she never truly fits in the relationships she creates, which makes her restless and dejected, stuck in her own cycle of transference, recreating her childhood pain.

THE FOSTER-CHILD HEART

People with foster-child hearts live in a state of fear, especially as they settle into new groups. Due to their past experiences, they feel as if they do not belong and work extremely hard to learn the rules of the group in an attempt to fit in. These individuals live with the expectation of being asked to leave at any moment. Foster-child hearts live in anxiety and fear of rejection—in their hearts, their bags are already packed.

Sarah also has this kind of heart. She is always struggling to learn the rules of the new relationships that she finds herself in, frantically trying to grasp what she can do to earn the validation of the men she admires. She battles an inherent sense of worthlessness instead of turning to the Holy Spirit to adopt the areas of her heart that lie dormant and empty.

THE SLAVE HEART

Finally, there are those who have faced trauma and live with slave hearts. These people feel there is no hope for them. They subconsciously live life as if someone owns them, thus there is no hope for freedom. They live in a seemingly inescapable mental poverty caused by their trauma. Their victim mentality has trapped them.

Someone with a slave heart believes that their life has been controlled by others and they have no voice. They do not trust others and live life as if there were no escape from the pain. They live in emotional poverty and are angry that they have been treated unjustly. When one experiences the orphan, step-child, foster-child, or slave heart, life seems meanliness. When we have these kinds of hearts, whether we know it or not, our barn is burning. Everything we've so painstakingly tried to build inside our four walls becomes meaningless when we look at the Holy Spirit and how we can be taken out of our self-imposed limits. Our works and achievements distract us so that we don't even see the flames needing immediate attention.

These flames represent our trauma, and they start with a small spark that grows into a tiny flame. But our barns are flammable, filled with wood and hay, just as we ourselves are fragile because we have not developed, or fully developed our identity and purpose. Individuals with any of the four hearts live life searching for people, or situations to fill the holes in their heart. There is a direct correlation between the condition of our hearts and the state of our spiritual homes—our hearts need to be in the right place before we can address our barns.

We can leave our barns behind when we accept God's offer of adoption. What does it mean to accept being adopted into the Kingdom of God? The act of adoption is defined as legally taking another's child and bringing it up as one's own. When God says he wants to adopt us, the first thing we need to understand is the weight of that offer. Ephesians 1:5 (NLT) says that "God decided in advance to adopt us into his own family by bringing us to Himself through Jesus Christ. This is what he wanted to do, and it gave him great delight." Although our sin has separated us from God, we have been offered a chance to re-enter into a relationship with him by accepting his offer of adoption through Jesus Christ. This offer is huge, great news for us. God gave his only son so that we may be forgiven of our sins and brought back into relationship with him.

If spiritual adoption by God is such a great deal, why do we run away from it? The answer goes back to trauma, as we've discussed previously. The pain of trauma holds us back from fully accepting God during our struggle to work through the emotional and physical hurt we've experienced at the hands of others. We relate our expectations and trust in humans to our expectations and trust in God. However, these two relationships cannot be equated, for God is ever righteous and good, whereas humans will always fall short.

TYPES OF TRAUMA

We must consider two types of trauma when we look at why people push away the offer of adoption from God. Firstly, there is A-trauma. This kind of trauma occurs when there is an absence of good things in our childhoods. Essentially, the traumatic experience has occurred from a lack of action rather than a deliberate action. A-trauma can be difficult to identify because we often think about what has happened to us when we think about our transference, but sometimes the question that needs to be asked is what *didn't* happen to us?

Sarah would be an example of someone experiencing the effects that cause the cycle of transference. A-trauma is like carbon monoxide poisoning; you cannot see or smell the abuse. Sarah never received the affirmation and love that she longed for in her childhood. She lacked a father figure who would have consistently offered unconditional parental love to her, and now she finds herself seeking that fatherly love in other men. What Sarah will come to realize is that the father figure she seeks is entirely available to her at any time provided she accepts the offer of adoption. Sarah's problem, of course, is that deep down she has a core belief that God the Father won't provide the unconditional love she is seeking. She can't bring herself to trust that God will give her all the love she needs, and thus, she remains in her cycle of pain due to A-trauma.

The second type of trauma is B-trauma, which is denoted by a physical, literal action or event that occurred in someone's life (likely during childhood) and has caused profound emotional damage. B-trauma events are easier to spot because you have experienced the physical and emotional abuse from your offender. It's often easier to trace back behavior to a specific event than it is to search for what is missing.

Jake is experiencing a B-trauma separation from a relationship with God. The action of being abandoned by a parental figure has led Jake to believe that God will abandon him as well. Jake believes no one will be a constant presence and companion in his life. He is making the mistake of equating his relationship and experience with humans to the kind of experiences and relationships that he can have with God. These two relationships are entirely different, but Jake's trauma tells him they are the same.

This kind of trauma response is indicative of the heart of a victim or a survivor. When we are incapable of accepting the invitation of adoption from God, we cut ourselves off from what is offered to us and situate ourselves in our barns. As we have learned, our barns are flammable, fragile, but a relationship with God never will be.

THE OVERCOMER HEART

We can now begin to talk about what the heart of an overcomer looks like. An overcomer understands acceptance and adoption offered by God. We give up being too easily pleased, being content in our well-insured barns, and we enter into a new closeness with God. We transition from survivor to overcomer.

Overcomers' hearts are different in two ways: their relationship with God and their relationships with those around them. The acceptance of adoption brings their heart closer to the Father through the Holy Spirit. Their relationship with God is stronger than ever before—and they have fostered a deep connection between themselves and the creator of the universe.

Overcomers' hearts change the way they treat the people around them. Cycles of transference end and they find contentment and love in the Father. God begins to heal their trauma as they trust in and begin to build a relationship with him. No longer do they inadvertently use other people or hurt themselves in a response to trauma. All of this is possible when we choose to accept the invitation that God has given us to join his family. If we turn to God instead of ourselves or other things then, our souls will be healed permanently and we can move from a survivor to an overcomer.

3

PROGRAMMED OR PURPOSEFUL?

Therefore, if anyone is in Christ, the new creation has come; the old has gone, the new is here.

—2 Corinthians 5:17 NIV

It's time to start asking ourselves if we are programmed or purposeful. We can begin to answer this question by thinking about something we are familiar with: a computer. Computers run on software, which naturally, needs to be updated frequently. Most people now have smartphones, which offer new software updates almost once a year. When we don't update our phones and computers, they become sluggish. Apps run slower, new applications can't load because the hardware requires the new software. Humans are similar to computers in this way. We need to keep our software up to date and ask ourselves, "Are we being programmed, or purposeful?"

Think back to the types of hearts that we talked about in the previous section: orphan, stepchild, foster-child, and slave hearts. All of these are considered "old software." These kinds of hearts or mindsets are outdated because they are not who we are anymore. We have the Holy Spirit now, and thus have been made new. If we open our hearts and minds and are willing to follow the Holy Spirit, we are running on the updated software made available to us.

So what is this new software update we're being offered? The Holy Spirit offers us new life when we put our faith in Jesus Christ. We are being offered a chance to be made brand new—just as an old phone becomes "new" when we launch an update. Our software is renewed the same way when we allow God to do updates on us. 2 Corinthians 5:17 ESV says, "If we are in Christ, we are made new." Gone are our orphan hearts and slave hearts. We have been gifted the opportunity to be the absolute best we can be, as close to the original version as God intended. All we have to do is accept the update.

No one can move from survivor to overcomer without the Holy Spirit. It is impossible to download the software necessary for healing and overcoming without the help of the Lord. God is always offering to take us on a journey from a broken existence to a whole one, to one that is brand new and functions as it was always meant to—in a close relationship with him. Consider again the idea of being too easily pleased. Would you accept slow software on your computer when free, fast, and reliable software is readily available?

When we accept ideas such as being a survivor is all we will ever be, we are stubbornly making our own lives more difficult by continuing to run out-of-date software. Refusing to update gets us no closer to being an overcomer. To be an overcomer, we must delete the programs that we have grown accustomed to using and decide to be purposeful with our actions.

With a better understanding of the terms *programmed* and *purposeful*, we can ask ourselves whether we are living in an old program. Are we accepting ourselves as victims or survivors and refusing the update to be an overcomer? It is impossible to live up to our full potential when we approach life in this way. To accept this new way of life, we must self-sacrifice, that is, take our identity out of the survivor mentality. It is only by choosing to accept the offer being given to us that we can truly live our lives with purpose. We need the newest software available to run our absolute best, and God is offering that to us.

GENERATIONAL PATTERNS AND CURSES

Why is it important to accept the new programming? Generational curses threaten our health. Referencing the computer analogy, they're like viruses. Generational curses are patterns that originate from beliefs and actions repeated from one generation to the next. Some of these family patterns are healthy and helpful, but these patterns may also be harmful to our spiritual, emotional, and physical health. Eventually, these unhealthy family patterns form the foundation of a child's development, and ultimately, become truth to them.

Generational patterns become generational curses only when we fail to recognize them and intentionally act to counter them. These curses are activated by the choices we make. An example of this would be the pattern of alcoholism. In such families, there is a genetic predisposition to alcoholism. Family members have a choice. They may choose to abstain from alcohol, drink occasionally, or avoid all parameters. How they choose to treat alcohol is entirely dependent upon them. They have a chance to stop a generational curse or perpetuate it further.

Generational curses are by no means a matter of fairness. Each family grapples with its own struggles and issues, and generational curses are often inconsistent. They can skip generations and seemingly disappear for many years before suddenly reemerging. For example, a man may struggle with alcoholism, but we don't see the struggle again until it reappears in his great-grandson. These curses can be difficult to recognize because of this delay, which is why being purposeful, rather than programmed, is so important.

BURIED BENEATH THE SURFACE

A good way of understanding generational curses is to compare them to the life of a tulip. When you plant a tulip bulb, and care for it and nurture it under the right conditions, it grows: first as a stem, then leaves, and eventually the part we know to be the flower. Tulips are perennials, meaning if you leave the bulbs in the ground after they've bloomed and died, they will return in the following year and start the process all over again. As long as the conditions are right (good soil, lots of sunlight, and plenty of water), the bulb multiplies and produces more flowers the next year,

It's our choice as to whether we provide the right conditions for sin to grow. We can't do anything about the bulbs. They were here before we were born. However, we can cultivate conditions that grow the tulips or starve the tulip. What we do with the environment is something each of us needs to own.

If generational sin is inherent and rooted within our families, what can we do about it? The logical answer would be to dig up the roots of these issues—to take the time to fully understand and address the deeper level of the problem. Often, though, instead of doing this, we find ourselves simply hacking at the flowers with shears—momentarily solving the problem but never addressing the root of the sin. This is where barn building begins. Victim and survivor mentalities take over and we try to fix the issues ourselves despite our inability to get to the issues' core. We must take that step of adoption and ask God to help us root out our generational sins.

What matters, however, is that we ourselves facilitate these actions with our own choices. Generational sin continues because of our conscious choices. It's essential we choose to be purposeful and not programmed in our lives. When we allow ourselves to be programmed and run on old software, we easily become lost in our sin and fall into generational habits we are predisposed to. Thus, being purposeful in our obedience to God and his word is the necessary step for moving from survivor to overcomer.

God desires for his children to walk close to him. One of the reasons for this is protection. Just as a good parent warns their children not to do things that could cause harm to them, God warns us to be obedient because he loves us and wants the best for his children.

Any loving and caring parent will teach their child how to safely cross an intersection. This is for their own protection because someday, your child will need to cross a busy intersection without your help. If, after doing all you possibly can to properly instruct your child, one day your child darts out onto the road and almost gets hit by a car, did you fail or did your child fail to follow your directions? God's laws are for preventing us from being hit by the effects of sin. A generational curse is caused by the effects of sin and is a consequence of disobedience. The purpose of a curse is to get your attention so you can make the choice to do things differently. This means doing things God's way. As do most loving parents, God truly knows what's best for us.

We see examples of generational sins and curses when we turn to the Bible as well. Beginning in Genesis, we see the effects of generational curses on Abraham and the generations that follow. Abraham went to Egypt to live because of a severe famine in the land. Upon his arrival, he began a generational pattern of deceit and selfishness that carried through his generation and those to come. In Genesis, Abraham said, "I just assumed that there was no fear of God in this place and that they'd kill me to get my wife. Besides, the truth is that she is my half sister; she's my father's daughter but not my mother's. When God sent me out as a wanderer from my father's home, I told her, 'Do me a favor; wherever we go, tell people that I'm your brother.' Then Abimelech gave Sarah back to Abraham, and along with her sent sheep and cattle and servants, both male and female. He said, 'My land is open to you; live wherever you wish'" (Genesis 20:11-16, NKJV). By lying about his relationship with Sarah, Abraham set an example for his generations to follow.

Even though Abraham's son Isaac was not yet born at the time of this sin, a seed was sown in these sins that would affect him. Isaac's son Jacob would eventually come to deceive his father in order to gain his father's blessing that belonged to his older brother Esau. In this family, there was never any root confrontation of the generational curse. Generational curses come from the process of spiritual sowing and reaping—whatever sin pattern you sow will be passed down from generation to generation until the sin pattern is addressed properly through intentional purpose and relationship with God.

Understanding generational curses is imperative to understanding why we have a separation between victim, survivor, and overcomer mentalities. When we are stuck in the victim or survivor categories, we are still being ruled by our generational patterns and sins. We have yet to fully trust God and accept the relationship he offers us—we remain in cycles of transference that reach all the way back through the generations. We must ask ourselves if we're being programmed or purposeful in our everyday life and make the necessary changes to remove our old software and download the upgrade we are offered by the love of God.

4

MEANT FOR MORE

My grace is always more than enough for you.

—2 Corinthians 12:9 NIV

Now that we know more about trauma, what does it mean to truly move from victim or survivor to overcomer? The question to ask yourself is which of the three does my life represent? Progressing from one mentality to the next requires that we understand the differences between the three categories and learn how we identify ourselves within each category. Our reactions to offenses or wounds determine whether we are victims, survivors, or overcomers. As we live in a world of sin, we react to these sins by choosing to be a victim, survivor, or overcomer. And, yes, it is a choice! How we *choose* to react to what wounds us determines a plethora of things: our relationships with people, our perspectives, and our relationship with God. There are three ways that we can choose to respond to trials in our lives:

1. The victim mentality.
   You refuse to take responsibility. Everything in life is not your fault and other people and circumstances are to blame.
2. The survivor mentality.
   You believe that you do not need help. You have everything under control yet become angry when no one offers to help.
3. The overcomer mentality.
   You know that God's got your back and with Him at your side you can walk through the circumstances of life.

THE VICTIM

First, let's review what a victim is in a spiritual context. We may describe a victim as a person who, individually or collectively, has suffered harm, including physical or mental injury, emotional suffering, economic loss, or substantial impairment of their fundamental rights, through acts or omissions in violation of laws operative within member states, including those proscribing criminal abuse of power. The world is full of victims. You can probably think of many just in your life alone. Recognizing you are in a victim mentality is the first step to moving onto a survivor mentality, not where we ultimately want to be, but one step closer to that overcomer we are longing to be.

A victim's motto is "You owe me." Victims are recognizable by certain traits and lifestyles. Victims live in a world of confusion. Their traumatic events have defined who they are, which leads to confusion and frustration as they begin to seek their identity and purpose outside of that trauma. Due to this confusion, victims start to mold themselves into what society tells them to be. Victims struggle with transference and projection more than the other two mentalities as they struggle to understand their role and purpose in life and in relationships. Victims also tend to struggle to take responsibility for their own healing since they are stuck in a blame game with who or what happened to them rather than taking action to allow themselves to heal.

We find a biblical example of a victim in the story of the prodigal son. In this story, it is the brother of the prodigal who is stuck in a victim mentality. He saw himself as only a victim of circumstance and refused to recognize or remove himself from that mentality. The story goes as follows:

> Then Jesus said, "Once there was a father with two sons. The younger son came to his father and said, 'Father, don't you think it's time to give me my share of your estate?' So, the father went ahead and distributed between the two sons their inheritance. Shortly afterward, the younger son packed up all his belongings and traveled off to see the world. He journeyed to a far-off land where he soon wasted all he was given in a binge of extravagant and reckless living. With everything spent

and nothing left, he grew hungry, because there was a severe famine in that land. So, he begged a farmer in that country to hire him. The farmer hired him and sent him out to feed the pigs. The son was so famished, he was willing even to eat the slop given to the pigs, because no one would feed him a thing. Humiliated, the son finally realized what he was doing, and he thought, 'There are many workers at my father's house who have all the food they want with plenty to spare. They lack nothing. Why am I here dying of hunger, feeding these pigs, and eating their slop? I want to go back home to my father's house, and I'll say to him, "Father, I was wrong. I have sinned against you. I will never again be worthy to be called your son. Please, Father, just treat me like one of your employees."' So, the young son set off for home. From a long distance away, his father saw him coming, dressed as a beggar, and great compassion swelled up in his heart for his son who was returning home. The father raced out to meet him, swept him up in his arms, hugged him dearly, and kissed him over and over with tender love. Then the son said, "Father, I was wrong. I have sinned against you. I could never deserve to be called your son. Just let me be—" The father interrupted and said, "Son, you're home now!" Turning to his servants, the father said, "Quick, bring me the best robe, my very own robe, and I will place it on his shoulders. Bring the ring, the seal of sonship, and I will put it on his finger. And bring out the best shoes you can find for my son. Let us prepare a great feast and celebrate" (Luke 15:11-24 NIV).

So, what is the older brother's response to all of this? He sees that his brother has returned after years of behaving irresponsibly, only to be welcomed back and honored as if he had been a perfectly behaved son during his absence. Instead of being glad that a relationship had been mended, the brother turned to anger against his younger brother and father. Because he is in a victim mentality, the brother plays the blame game. He treats his father and brother poorly, and when questioned why, he lays the blame on the others' actions. When he refuses to join the celebration of his brother's return, he makes excuses rather than taking ownership of his emotions and actions. He deflects any responsibility for his angry response by refusing to claim any fault for himself, by demanding an apology.

A victim mentality is common and it's easy for people to become stuck in it. Victims often suffer difficult emotions after traumatic events that cause them to behave in these manners. They become frustrated and angry with a world that seems against them, hopeless about their never changing circumstances. They settle for hurt, believing loved ones do not care, and they are resentful of happy and successful people. Some victims may subconsciously blame others for the problems they cause, lash out and make others feel guilty, or manipulate others to gain sympathy and attention. Victims can be difficult, and they are often unaware of the reason behind their actions.

In order to shift from victim to survivor, the victim must consciously understand and accept their condition and then decide to leave that mentality.

Victims sometimes realize on their own they want a healthier, happier way of life and begin to make this transition. Rather than aiming to be an overcomer, though, their goal is to simply achieve survivor status. After all, much of society views survivors as victors of trauma, and thus, many stay content.

THE SURVIVOR

Survivors, despite being a step up from a victim, are still a step short of an overcomer. Society tells us being a survivor is the final stop and that there is no other goal to reach once we're at this point. Of course, we know from the Bible this isn't true. We are meant for more than we could possibly imagine. Before we focus on overcomers, let's review the definition of a survivor.

Survivors cope with bad situations or afflictions and get through them. Perhaps they even live through a situation that causes death. We hear of crazy survival stories on TV and on the internet all the time—someone who survived a fifty-foot fall or miraculously escaped unscathed from a shark attack. Rarely, though, do we hear about survivors of every day, almost mundane traumas that people struggle with. The news doesn't show a clip of your neighbor struggling with a gambling addiction, or your cousin enduring an emotionally abusive marriage. These types of traumatic events are silent, yet the survivors of these events are no less survivors than those who experience catastrophic accidents.

A survivor's motto is, "Pull yourself up by your bootstraps.". Survivors tend to judge themselves harshly as they believe only they can pull themselves out of the struggles they face. They have a well-built barn, one full of helpful tools and food. Yet, they remain unaware of how flammable that barn is. Survivors spend a lot of time trying to understand why the event that harmed them happened. They have moved on from the blame game and have put the role of healing entirely on themselves, and thus search for answers, subconsciously hoping to take control of their situation. Survivors are quick to resent God, and they begin to ask, "Why did God allow that to happen?" They judge themselves, and they judge God in hopes of understanding. Finally and most importantly, survivors do not want or think they need help. Society has told them that if they can get themselves to a certain point of understanding and healing, they will be fixed and can move on with their lives.

The problem with this process is that it entirely overlooks the fact that a survivor mentality is nothing more than the idolatry of the self in disguise. Believing we are fully capable of spiritual and emotional healing without the help of God is false and an act of disobedience against God. Believing we are good enough on our own is where many fall short and become stuck in the survivor mentality. It isn't difficult to understand how this happens when we have a world around us telling us otherwise. The world generally does not support a victim mentality, but it surely loves a survivor mentality. The key to moving beyond this step is understanding the difference between survivor and overcomer in the eyes of God.

THE OVERCOMER

In the Bible, Job illustrates an example of someone able to move from survivor to overcomer. Perhaps no character has suffered more than Job. He had everything—a wonderful family, a good name, and plenty of wealth. But then Satan went to God seeking permission to alter Job's good fortune.

Tragedy struck and Job lost everything: his children, his wealth, his livestock, his crops, his health, and even his relationship with his wife and friends. And what did Job do? He didn't curse God, as Satan had thought he would. Instead, he praised God's name.

> At this, Job got up and tore his robe and shaved his head. Then he fell to the ground in worship and said: "Naked I come from my mother's womb, and naked I will depart. The Lord gave and the Lord has taken away; may the name of the Lord be praised. (Job 1:20-21NT)

Job questioned God, but he remained humbled. His motto was, "With God's help, I will overcome." He didn't give up. Rather, he seriously considered, "How can I keep going?" Job eventually repents and constantly stays humble before God.

At the beginning of this story, we see Job in a survivor mentality. He faces hardship and trauma in his life and questions God, trying to understand the reasons for his suffering. We learn it is okay to question God. It's okay not to have the answers. Our job is to put our ultimate trust and understanding in God. The difference between survivors and overcomers is where they put their trust and hope for a better tomorrow. Survivors choose themselves. Overcomers choose Christ and the Holy Spirit.

The Greek word most often translated as "overcomer" originates from the word *Nike* which, according to *Strong's Concordance*, means "to carry off the victory." What makes an overcomer? Overcomers understand they cannot save themselves, rather, they need God to save them from themselves.

> "For whatever is born of God overcomes the world; and this is the victory that has overcome the world—our faith. Who is the one who overcomes the world, but he who believes that Jesus is the Son of God?" (1 John 5:4 NIV)

True overcomers understand this and live by it. These people are followers of Christ who successfully resist the power and temptation of the world's system. Survivors are who the world wants them to be. Overcomers are who God wants them to be. As God's children, we are meant for more than what the world tells us to be.

Overcomers are not sinless. Rather, they hold fast to faith in Christ until the end. Overcomers have trauma. They have challenges and hardships and failures just like victims and survivors. The key difference is they have put their faith and trust in Jesus to lead them through spiritual healing. Overcoming requires complete dependence upon God for direction, purpose, fulfillment, and strength to follow his plan for our lives. Overcoming requires us to humble ourselves to hold God up higher. It takes removing the focus on ourselves and putting it back on the Father.

Overcomers are learners. They began as victims and survivors just like everyone else. They felt the same hopelessness and loss we've felt. They've experienced frustration and confusion too. They've asked the same questions and felt just as lost. What they changed, however, wasn't so much asking questions but asking the *right* questions. Rather than trying to heal themselves, they seek healing through Jesus. These are the kind of questions that true overcomers ask:

- What does **God** want?
- What works and what can I **learn**?
- What am I **assuming** and what are the facts?
- What am I **missing**? What are my choices?
- What action steps make the best **sense**?
- What is **possible**?

Overcomers understand that when they turn their questions to be Christ-focused rather than self-focused, they maintain the mindset of an overcomer. They have learned to not focus on the previous or future seasons of life, but to love and trust in the present season where God has placed them.

We were never designed to stay comfortable in a victim or survivor lifestyle. We have been made new by Christ's love. It's our responsibility to move closer to him and become overcomers.

FIVE STEPS TO GO FROM VICTIM OR SURVIVOR TO OVERCOMER

1. **Own the problem.** Taking ownership of our problems is the first step to becoming an overcomer. We don't control what happens to us, but we always control our response. In hardship and struggle, we own our problems by accepting them and giving them to God, then asking for guidance to implement a Christ-like response to them.

2. **Don't keep secrets.** Give yourself wholly and entirely to God. Don't try to hide your fears and failures from him. Instead, turn to him for help and guidance. This is difficult when we feel we have been hurt or that no one can understand our pain. Remember, Jesus took every pain that could ever be felt for us on the cross. If anyone truly knows how you feel in your trauma and pain, it is God.

3. **Allow God to heal the roots of your painful issues.** We need to give God access to the core of our pain. In addition to not keeping secrets, we must open up to God and not bury the pain we experience. When we show him our wounds, we can trust that God will

heal them, not cause more damage to the hurt already present.

4. **Walk in authentic forgiveness.** Forgive those around you. Forgive those who have hurt you, those who will hurt you, and those who are currently hurting you. Forgive yourself for your own shortcomings and ask for forgiveness from God as well. (See sample prayers for forgiveness in the Appendix.)

5. **Let go of inner vows and bitterly rooted judgments.** Our vows and judgments are not the vows and judgments of God. We need to release what we hold in our hearts to make room for the things God tells us to keep in our hearts—we need to put God's wants and needs before our own in order to be overcomers.

As we move from victims and survivors to overcomers, it is important to remember we are meant for more. We are meant to learn to recognize transference and projection from victims and help others to recognize them too. We are meant to not be so easily pleased—we are meant to ask for more from God and receive blessings unimagined. We are meant to leave our barns and enter the Kingdom of Heaven. We are meant to be purposeful followers of Christ, guided by the Holy Spirit, rather than beings running on old programming and software. We are meant for so much more than we think, and when we accept that invitation of adoption, we can and will feel an unending joy in our lives.

5

JOURNEY TO UNENDING JOY™

For it was always in his perfect plan to adopt us as his delightful children, through our union with Jesus, the Anointed One, so that his tremendous love that cascades over us would glorify his grace—for the same love he has for his Beloved One, Jesus, he has for us. And this unfolding plan brings him great pleasure!

—Ephesians 1:5 NIV

When we accept God's offer of adoption and move from victims and survivors to overcomers, we will receive an incredible offer of a joyful life. Living for God and not for ourselves ensures that we put God's plans first and we implicitly trust in his ways. A joyful existence is what is promised to us when we accept God's hand that is always extended to us. Kay Warren writes in her book *Choose Joy,* "Joy is the settled assurance that God is in control of all the details of my life." She goes on to say "Joy is the quiet confidence that ultimately everything is going to be alright." I like to believe that Joy is understanding that God has a plan and when we ask he will direct our paths through the valley of turmoil.

The Journey to Unending Joy™, however, is exactly that—a journey. It is a journey that begins with choosing joy. This takes time, effort, and all of the work that comes with maintaining a relationship with someone you love deeply. Firstly, the shift to becoming an overcomer will take time because we do not become perfect overcomers overnight. Time can be a frustrating character, for it often seems that it moves quickly while we make little progress at what we are working so hard to achieve. We need to wake up each day understanding that sometimes we will fail to be an overcomer in our actions and feelings, but that we will continue to try—no matter what.

Next our choice is to pursue unending joy. We must actively pursue a relationship with God, meaning we are praying, communicating, reading scripture, and leaning on other followers of Jesus for guidance. God says he will meet us where we are in our healing journey, but once he has met us where we are, it is our responsibility to put in the effort just as we would in any other loving relationship. We can take things we filled our barns with, such as memorizing scripture and church attendance and meditation, and rather than performing them to make ourselves feel better, use them to bring ourselves closer in our relationship with God.

Finally, we need to choose joy in our journey. There will be days when we struggle to be an over-comer, days when we feel more like a victim. Healing is not linear. God is with us through it all should we choose to accept the help we desperately need. We can experience the pure joy that comes with growing closer to the Lord, even when we are in a painful time in our life. A relationship with God is the source of unending joy that we are seeking. It is the only way to truly heal and become who God intended us to be.

It is important to recognize that we may be on different legs of our journeys at different times of our lives. There will be times when we are victims, times when we are survivors, and times when we are overcomers. These mindsets are neither fixed nor mutually exclusive, and often, we can be all three at once in different areas of our lives.

Perhaps we have managed to be overcomers in our troubled relationships with our parents, but remain a victim of our addictions. We can be an overcomer and stop putting in the effort and revert back to a victim at any time, just as we can realize we are idolizing ourselves and begin to put Christ first again. When we include God and keep him as a part of the process, he can guide us back to being overcomers whenever we slip and fall back into old habits. As we build our relationship with God, we begin to feel the joy that comes with loving the creator of the universe as closely as an intimate friend—an unending joy that will stay with us forever.

THE TRUTH YOUR LIFE CAN BE BUILT ON

Our friends Jake and Sarah have come to realize their statuses as victims and survivors and have worked to become overcomers. Sarah dug deeper into her A-trauma with a counselor and confided in God with a cry for help and healing. Over time, she began to feel the joy that came with her finding a never-failing father figure, and for the first time in her life, felt truly loved. Jake began to grapple with his B-trauma and focused on the Lord rather than himself. He learned that by trying to maintain his survivor status he was missing how God needed to be central in his healing process. He became purposeful about the activities he was doing already, like going to church every week, centering that time on God and building a relationship with him.

Both Sarah and Jake still slip up at times—afterall, they are human and can never be perfect. They are on a long journey to joy that starts with a dedication to having an overcomer mindset. There are noticeable differences in their hearts and in their actions as they've accepted God's offer of adoption and have tasted some of the joy offered to us.

All of us are capable of being overcomers. The invitation is extended to all. No one is too far gone or too hurt to come back to God, to accept all that is offered to us in our time here on Earth. When we refuse to be too easily pleased and settle for what the world offers us, we are pursuing God's wants and wishes for us. When we turn our backs on our barns for the Kingdom of God, we are trusting God to catch us when we take that leap of faith. When we make our lives purposeful, we are acting as stewards of faith and pleasing God. Finally, when we believe in our hearts that we are meant for more and chase after that joyful relationship with God, we are on the path to living a righteous life as overcomers, one that will guide us to the very end of our time here.

Take a moment to reflect upon the title of the book, The Lie your Life is Based On. Throughout our time together, were there any lies that surfaced into your awareness?

Perhaps the lie I was wired this way. I cannot change. I need to accept suffering in my life.

Remember, acceptance of pain does not bring change. Pain is inevitable, but suffering is optional. Overcomers pursue Kingdom Joy and understand that His joy is our backbone that lifts our soul and spirit. Kingdom Joy is activated whenever we rejoice. To rejoice in the Lord always is not an emotion but an activation of the unending joy we are given at salvation. When we understand our identity as overcomers, we can experience firsthand that "His Joy comes in the morning." (See Psalms 30:5)

The lie most of us build our lives on is that we can save ourselves and that survivor is the best we can hope for. The truth is we can't save ourselves, but through the Holy Spirit's power we can transform into overcomers and achieve our divine destiny.

Review the Journey to Unending Joy™ chart below. Compare and contrast each category.

Victim	Survivor	Overcomer
"I won't grow up"	"I'm a survivor"	"I shall overcome"
Drowning in Water	Treading in Water	Walking on Water
Living Dead	Life	Abundant Life
Unprotected	Self-Protected	Protected
Orphan	Step Child	Adopted Son or Daughter
Ghetto	Suburbs	Palace
Past	Future	Present
Child	Teenager	Adult
Not able to love	Too busy to love	Able to love unconditionally
Unforgiveness	Acceptance	Forgiveness
Generational Curses	Personal Achievements	Spiritual Inheritance
Never Dreams	Sometimes Dreams	Always Dreams
Poor	Middle Class	Royalty
Loner	Lonely	Never Alone
Lie	Half Truth	Truth
Situational Joy	Happiness	Unending Joy

APPENDIX

The Process of True Forgiveness

1. Ask the Holy Spirit to reveal the details concerning <u>one specific event.</u>
2. Confess to Jesus <u>what took place</u> (the event).
3. Confess <u>how you felt</u> (what your heart felt at the time of the offense).
4. Now confess to Jesus <u>what you thought</u> (what your head thinks).
5. Did you do anything in revenge or to get even? This includes holding onto bitterness. Seek forgiveness.

Sample Healing Prayer

- Let go of your <u>emotions</u> (one by one) concerning this one event. Say, "Jesus, <u>I let go</u> of my (fear, anger, rejection, etc.) and place the emotion at the cross."
- Did you make any <u>inner vows</u>? If so, say "I confess the inner vow that _____. I ask

you Jesus to forgive me for this belief. I choose to forgive myself. Now sever this vow with the sword of the Spirit and I choose to believe _____ (the truth/the opposite) ."

- Did you make any <u>bitter root judgments</u>? If so, say "I confess the bitter root judgment that _____ . I ask you Jesus to forgive me for this belief. I choose to forgive myself. Now I sever this judgment with the sword of the Spirit and choose to believe _____ (the truth/the opposite) ."

- Did you do anything in revenge or to get even? If so, say "I confess my reaction was not godly. Jesus, I ask you to forgive me for _____."

- <u>Now forgive the person for this one event</u>. Say, "Jesus I choose to forgive _____ (person's name) _____ for _____. I choose to set them free, and I am set free." Be sure to repent of your own bitterness, etc.

Prayer to Break Inner Vows

Inner Vows begin with the word I.

Proverbs 23:7 (NKJV) Example: I will never love again. I will not trust.

Father in the Name of Jesus, I confess I created a vow that was pain driven. I realize the vow prevents me from moving in life. I break the Inner Vow _____ in Jesus Christ Name. I chose to believe _____.

Prayer to Break Bitter Root Judgement.

Matthew 7: 1-2 (NIV)

Bitter root judgments prevent others from blessing you. Example: People will mock me when...

Father in the name of Jesus Christ, I confess I created a judgment from my heart of bitterness. I ask you to forgive me for believing _____.
By your blood Jesus Christ I break that vow and chose to believe _____.

Prayer to Forgive Others

Matthew 6:14-15 (NIV)

Father through the Holy Spirit you have revealed to me that I am holding on to pain because I have not forgiven (name) _____. I no longer want the unforgiveness in my heart to keep me in bondage. In the Name of Jesus Christ, I chose to forgive _____. Please forgive me for the vows and judgments I made during the painful events.

Prayer to Break Generational Curses

Deuteronomy 5:9b-10 (NKJV)

Father, the Holy Spirit has revealed to me that I need to cut off a generational sin pattern of (name the pattern) . I have chosen to walk in the same pattern and thus remain a victim of the sins of my family. I forgive my father's (Mother) family for not obeying your word and brought this curse into my life. By the Power of the Blood of Jesus Christ I severe the sin pattern of _____. I make a choice to be obedient to your word so the generations after me will be blessed.

Prayer of Adoption

(Romans 8:15-17 NIV)

Father, I have been searching for the feeling I belong to a family and others. I now know that the Holy Spirit will fill that void in my heart with your Father's love. I choose to embrace the love you have for me and not to reject you. In the name of the Father, The Son and The Holy Spirit fill that empty place with your love until it overflows. I will embrace your love by walking with you on a daily basis. Fill me Holy Spirit with the Spirit of adoption and joy.

ABOUT THE AUTHOR

Pastor Sandy Burkett, Ph.D. has been a full-time pastoral counselor since 1980. She was ordained through Christian International and has a Ph.D. in Biblical Counseling from Trinity Theological Seminary. Her Ph.D. research was on the Restoration of Joy in Victims of Childhood Trauma. Dr. Sandy believes that the anointing of the Holy Spirit is more successful than book knowledge to help victims to be overcomers. As a Board Certified Pastoral Counselor (AACC), Dr. Sandy has ministered to those with Post Traumatic Stress Disorder, Dissociative Identity Disorder, cult-related issues, marriages, and those wanting freedom from sexual sins.

In 1987, God released a passion to equip those in churches to counsel the brokenhearted. Dr. Sandy understood that many broken people sought help from their family, friends, church leaders and pastors before they made an appointment with a professional counselor. Thus, BreakThrough Biblical Counseling training was written and at present the class is thirty weeks long. Breakthrough Biblical Counseling class has influenced churches to offer help to those wounded in their congregations. There have been over 2,000 graduates in the central Ohio area from many denominations and non-denominations that use what they learned in their churches.

Dr. Sandy is a sought-after speaker and minister in the United States and Internationally. Her ministry includes healing the hearts of those wounded plus teaching and activating the Prophetic Giftings of the Holy Spirit. She is published and has presented papers at the American Association of Christian Counselors and special conferences on Dissociative Identity Disorder. She preaches, teaches, and is known as one who brings joy wherever she goes. Her heart is passionate to bring healing using biblical truth to those wounded, to train them to do the work of the minister and to send individuals that are equipped to change lives.

ACKNOWLEDGEMENTS

Over the years I have been blessed with individuals who believed in me, who prophetically encouraged me to write the revelations God has given me. I thank each of you for being a voice of God in my life.

I especially thank my husband, Greg, for being my cheerleader and the best intercessor any wife could ask for. To my friends of 30-plus years, Joyce Brown, Toni King, and Laurie Cimoch: you brought me flowers, balloons, cards of encouragement, and most of all laughter during the journey of birthing a book. And a special thank you to all the Breakthrough Biblical Counseling graduates who kept asking, "Are you writing a book? You should!"

My parents, Dane and Thelma Coffindaffer, were amazing. At an early age, you taught me that nothing was impossible, to think outside the box, and to dream big. Forever your voices in my heart continue to remind me, "You are a Coffindaffer—that is who you are." Our home was filled with laughter as we sat around the dinner table sharing our day with each other. Joy was alive in our home no matter the circumstances at that time.

Thank you to the amazing Igniting Souls publishing team. God brought you into my life to help birth a dream.

GET EQUIPED TO DO THE WORK OF THE MINISTRY.

Find out more at:
BREAKTHROUGHMINISTRIES.ORG

CONNECT WITH SANDY

Follow her on your favorite social media platforms today.

BREAKTHROUGHMINISTRIES.ORG

INTERESTED IN FINDING OUT HOW TO START LIVING YOUR MOST ABUNDANT LIFE TODAY?

Sandy Burkett will show you how to break free from past emotional and situational patterns so that you can experience joy, hope, and purpose.

KEYNOTE SPEAKER

START THE CONVERSATION TODAY

BREAKTHROUGHMINISTRIES.ORG

Enjoy Sandy's Other Book.

AVAILABLE WHEREVER BOOKS ARE SOLD.

BLOCKCHAIN
VERIFIED IP™

Powered by Easy IP™

Made in the USA
Middletown, DE
29 October 2023

41526776R00046